# THINGS YOU DIDN'T LEARN IN SCHOOL

BY

LINWOOD E. STRAYHORN, JR

DORRANCE
PUBLISHING CO
EST. 1920
PITTSBURGH, PENNSYLVANIA 15238

Dorrance Publishing Co
585 Alpha Drive
Pittsburgh, PA 15238
Visit our website at *www.dorrancebookstore.com*

ISBN: 979-8-89027-160-0
eISBN: 979-8-89027-658-2

# THINGS YOU DIDN'T LEARN IN SCHOOL

A man of commerce is a man of peace. Once you af-
fect his business. He then becomes a man of war.
Once he has to defend himself. He will never be a
man of peace again.

# ACKNOWLEDGMENTS

I would like to thank my family
Dedicated to the memory of my grandfathers
Henry Brown (father's biological father)
Alfred O Stewart (father's stepfather)
John D Blunt (mother's father)

# United States Panics Depressions Recessions

## 1785-2008

THIS BOOK CAME ABOUT AS AN EFFORT TO GIVE insight and understanding about recessions, depressions and panics that have occurred in the history of the United States of America. I was curious about how they begin and end along with their definitions and their effects. Where their effects were felt the most, who was responsible and who resolved the problems they caused. So first I have to look at the definition of the words. The definition of recession is a temporary slowdown in economic activity; depression is a period of severe economic decline; panic is a mass alarm about the economy, often resulting in a depression.

I have found that recessions, depressions, and panics occur more that we think. In researching these economic downturn periods, we go through them then they pass. So through my studies I realized that this is a nature cycle in our economy that occurs from time to time. Wars, greed and speculators are surely some of the main factors that contribute to them but are not the only factors. So I hope this information will assist you in understanding how these cycles occur and how to deal with them when they occur.

The panic of 1785 lasted for three years, following the American Revolutionary War concluding economic prosperity. A reduction in available currency and credit caused a fall in price levels. The victory at Yorktown caused overexpansion and debts. A lack of sufficient commerce, American manufacture could not compete with Britain. Things became increasingly serious with insufficient interstate trade.

Britain would not agree to end their commercial treaty. Businesses fell in default with debtor.

The 1785 panic led to the development of a stronger government under the new Constitution. At this time John Hancock, the 7th President of the United States Congressional Assembly under the Articles of Confederation was very ill. So David Ramsey served from November 2, 1785 to May 12, 1786. Then Nathaniel Gorham served from May 15, 1786 to June 5, 1786. Nathaniel Gorham was voted the 8th president of the United States Congressional Assembly under the Articles of Confederation. He served from June 6, 1786 to November 5, 1786. Arthur St. Clair was the 9th president of the United States Congressional Assembly under the Articles of Confederation. Cyrus Griffin was the 10th and final president of the United States Congressional Assembly under the Articles of Confederation. The complete name of the articles was United States Congressional Assembly under the Articles of Confederation and Perpetual Union. Robert Morris was the Superintendent of Finance under the Continental Congress from 1784 to 1789.

The Panic of 1792 was a two-month credit crisis due to questionable activities of speculators against stock and securities held by the newly established First Bank of the United States, the Bank of New York by speculators like William Duer (a lawyer, developer and speculator) and Alexander Macomb (a land speculator and shipping magnate). The bank's overextended notes and discounts. While speculators attempted to drive the stock prices up, others tried to drive them down which caused a bank run. A bank run is when large group of people withdraw their money because they believe the bank might become bankrupt. Macomb and Duer were ruined. They both were thrown into prison for insider trading. William Duer was the first person to be sent to prison for insider trading. The Secretary of Treasury, Alexander Hamilton, under the new federal Constitution led by President George Washington provided hundreds of thousand of dollars in relief to the economy and returned the situation to normal with his intervention.

The Panic of 1796-1797 was a large commercial decline in Britain and the United States due to the downturn in the Atlantic credit markets. Problems with the land speculation downward spiral in Britain emerged in America. The depression deepened when the Bank of England suspended specie (gold and silver coins) payments February 1797, due to the great cost of the war between the French and the British. The actions The Bank of England took lead to the downturn of the coastal United States and the Caribbean financial and commercial markets.

At this time George Washington was the president from 1789-1797. John Adams became president at the beginning of the panic from 1797-1801. The crisis resulted in the United States Congress passing the Bankruptcy Act of 1800 which ended the panic. The Bankruptcy Act expired in 1803 and was repelled.

John Adams's four years were tense. He kept George Washington's cabinet, instead of creating his own cabinet. Oliver Wolcott, Jr. replaced Alexander Hamilton as Secretary of the Treasury. He became secretary under President Washington and served from February 3, 1795 to December 31, 1800. Intense disagreements between Alexander Hamilton and Thomas Jefferson over the foreign policy made it difficult for Adams. Hamilton favored the British and Jefferson favored the French. Their disputes over the foreign policy probably did not help matters.

The Depression of 1807 was caused by the embargo on the shipping industries exporting of goods to Europe in retaliation of the British attacking the ship the Chesapeake. Congress under President Thomas Jefferson passed the Embargo Act of 1807. The depression lasted for seven years. It devastated the shipping industries and also industries related to shipping. The Federalist Party, who did not support President Jefferson, was against the embargo. They allowed smuggling of goods in New England. Thomas Jefferson was president from 1801-1809. Albert Gallatin was appointed Treasury Secretary under President Jefferson. He served as secretary for thirteen years under Jefferson to James Madison.

The panic of 1819 was a failure of expansionary monetary policy that lasted for five years. The government borrowed a large sum of money to finance the War of 1812 causing stress on the banks reserves and led to suspension of payment during a recession. It caused widespread foreclosures, bankruptcies, unemployment and bank runs. The Second Bank of the United States slowed speculation in commodities and western lands. The southern and western states were affected the hardest. Legislative relief for debtors and protection for manufactures was enacted in several western states and things improved by 1823. James Madison was the president at the time of the War of 1812, from 1809 to 1817. Albert Gallatin was the Secretary of the Treasury also during the War of 1812. He was secretary from May 14, 1801 to February 3, 1814. James Monroe was the president at the time of the panic of 1819, from 1817 to 1825. William Harris Crawford was the Secretary of the Treasury from October 22, 1816 to March 6, 1825.

Albert Gallatin was instrumental in dealing with the financial difficulties of the time. The embargo and the War of 1812 created a large federal budget deficit. He had to reenact federalist taxes that he was severely against. He also issued bonds successfully which paid for the war.

In 1813 Gallatin resigned as Treasury Secretary to become the diplomat that negotiates the Treaty of Ghent. The treaty ended the War of 1812 between the British and the French.

The panic of 1837 was believed to be caused by President Andrew Jackson's executive orders. The Deposit Act was passed June 23, 1832 which ordered that the surplus of millions in the Treasury be reallocated to the states proportion to the states populations. The president also vetoed renewing the charter of the Second Bank of the United States, which resulted in the withdrawal of government funds. On July 11, 1836, President Jackson issued an executive order of the specie Circular Act of 1836 which required buyers of property to use gold and silver coinage rather than paper money. The process would work in this way a buyer of property would go to the bank and exchange paper money for specie (gold and silver coins) to purchase property. The president thought that this would stop speculation in the west. The Bank of England was uncomfortable with the increased flow of funds into the United States interior. The Bank of England introduced a tightened monetary policy to recover specie thought to be lost.

One month and a week before the panic of 1837 in March Martin Van Buren became president. He was blamed for the downturn in the economy, due to his refusal to get involved, the new president was blamed for the six-year depression that followed the panic. The United States was able to recover after the depression with the Tariff of 1842. During William Henry Harrison's presidential term, he was elected in 1840. From March 6, 1829 to March 3, 1841, there had been five Treasury Secretaries. Samuel Delucenna Ingham was Secretary of the Treasury from March 6, 1829 to June 20, 1831. Louis McLane served as secretary from August 8, 1831 to May 28, 1833. William John Duane was secretary from May 29, 1833 to September 22, 1833 and Roger Brooke Taney was secretary from September 23, 1833 to June 25, 1834. Levi Woodbury served as Treasury Secretary from July 1, 1834 to March 1841 under Presidents Andrew Jackson and Martin Van Buren.

Treasury Secretary Woodbury was partially to blame for the Panic of 1837. He and President Jackson thought a like. They believed in an independent treasury system which leads to the collapse. Woodbury realized after the collapse the treasury needs to secure their funds not to use the commercial banks for replenishment. Due to this realization, in 1846 the U.S Treasury was established under President Polk.

The Panic of 1857 was started with the decline in the purchasing of American agriculture products by Europe. With the decline, agricultural profit funds invested in the Ohio Life Insurance and Trust Co. was lost. The recession spread fast from the Ohio Valley to the northeastern money centers. The economic problems lasted about a year and a half, but the recovery was unequal. The depression affected the industrial northeast and the western states the hardest. The southern states were less affected, because the cotton business was doing very well.

The Supreme Court case of Dred Scott vs. Sandford may have added to the problem. The court's decision threatened to spread slavery through the western territories which caused the bonds of the east-west running railroads to lose value. The Tariff Act of 1857 lowered the tariff rate 20%. It was written by Congressional Southerners and supported by most economic interests nationwide but not by the north.

The Tariff of 1857 became a major source of contention between the north and the south. Economic conditions were the most important issue in the election of 1860. Slavery seemed to be a subsequent after thought. The problem with the north and south was more about economics than slavery.

President Franklin Pierce and President James Buchanan were considered the worse presidents we had to this date. They both sat idle dealing with the situation of slavery which was tearing the country apart. Franklin Pierce was the president from 1853 to 1857 and James Buchanan was the president from 1857 to 1861.

During the time between 1857 and 1860, the country had two different Secretaries of the Treasury. James Guthrie of Kentucky was secretary from March 7, 1853 to March 6, 1857. Howell Cobb of Georgia was the Secretary of the Treasury under James Buchanan from March 7, 1857 to 1860.

Black Friday panic of 1869 was the attempt of Jay Gould and Jim Fisk to corner the gold market. They tried to buy enough gold to control the supply and the price. President Grant ordered his Treasury Secretary George Boutwell to release government gold for sale to stop them, by doing so making the problem.

Treasury Secretary Boutwell reorganized the Treasury Department. He downsized the treasury staff by letting go unnecessary employees. He made changes in the Bureau of Printing and Engraving to protect against counterfeiters. The Treasury had a monthly surplus due to these changes. The debt was reduced by selling the gold surplus at weekly auctions for currency and buying back the war bonds with the paper money. If the policy had continued it would have paid the national debt in 25 years.

The Panic of 1873 was due to the failure of several banks, the New York Warehouse and Securities Company; Kenyon, Cox and Co.; E.W Clark & Co. Bank; and the famous Philadelphia banking firm Jay Cooke and Co. on September 18, 1873. The stock market closed for ten days and the economy was in crisis. Economic over-investing and overexpansion came from excessive railroad construction. The railroad crisis came at the end of more economic crisis. The money supply tightened in 1873 which caused the panic. When Richardson became the new Treasury Secretary, he issued greenbacks paper money to calm the banks. His actions eased the crisis.

President Grant's administration raised the national credit, reduced taxes and interest rates. He reduced inflation by vetoing the Inflation Bill in 1874, which eased the monetary crisis on Wall Street. Ulysses S. Grant was the president from 1869 to1877. George Sewall Boutwell of Massachusetts was the Secretary of the Treasury from March 12, 1869 to June 3, 1874. Then William Adams Richardson took over, as Secretary of the Treasury from March 17, 1873 to June 3, 1874.

The Panic of 1884 was a small crisis. The European gold reserves were depleted and the New York City National banks halted investments and called in outstanding loans. A larger crisis was prevented when the New York Clearing House helped banks from failing. However, 10,000 other smaller investment firms failed. Chester A. Arthur was the president from 1881 to 1885. Charles James Folger died in office. He was the Secretary of the Treasury from November 14, 1881 to September 4, 1884. Walter Quintin Gresham replaced him from September 5, 1884 to October 30, 1884 just a little over a month. Gresham took another position in government.

Then Hugh McCulloch of Indiana served under Presidents Abraham Lincoln and Andrew Johnson as their Secretary of the Treasury from March 9, 1865 to March 3, 1869. He became the Treasury Secretary once again under Presidents Chester A. Arthur and Grover Cleveland from October 31, 1884 to March 7, 1885. McCulloch continued fighting for currency back by gold warning that silver coinage should be used as backing currency.

The Panic of 1893 was a depression caused by the railroad over-building and bad railroad financing; this set off bank failures, the expansion driven by speculation in market. February 23, 1893 the Philadelphia and Reading Railroad had over-extended and wanted to file for bankrupt. People caused bank runs.

European investors would only take payment in gold depleting the gold reserves. Also the Sherman Silver Purchase Act and the McKinley tariff of 1890 are partially to blame. There was a run on gold supplies. Politically President Cleveland and the Democratic Party were blamed. They lost in the 1894 elections. By the Presidential elections of 1896 there was no way Republican William McKinley could lose. Benjamin Harrison was at the end of his term as president at the time of the depression. He was the president from 1889 to 1893. Grover Cleveland started his second term at the beginning of the depression. He was the president from 1893 to 1897. The panic lasted for three years. Charles William Foster, Jr. was the Treasury Secretary from February 45, 1891 to March 6, 1893. John Griffin Carlisle was the secretary from March 7, 1893 to March 5, 1897.

The Panic of 1896 was a small depression compared to other panics of the times in the United States. Concerns on a decrease in silver reserves affected the gold standard in the market and lead to deflation of commodities driving the stock market to lower levels. The National Bank of Illinois failure was one motivating factor. Things would start to turn around after the election of William McKinley in 1896. John Griffin Carlisle was the Treasury Secretary under President McKinley.

The Panic of 1901 was caused by Edward Henry Harriman attempting to monopolize with Northern Pacific Railroad, by doing so he would control the Chicago rail market. He was trying to buy up Northern Pacific stock to control the rails. James J. Hill struggled with Harriman over control of the stock. So James J. Hill partner with J.P. Morgan to stop E.H. Harriman and his partner Jacob Schiff from gaining control of the stock. The struggle caused the New York Stock Exchange to crash for the first time.

James Stillman and William Rockefeller orchestrated the whole cornering the market of the stock financed with Standard Oil money. They all compromised and formed the Northern Securities Company. Thousands of small investors were ruined due to the crash. It occurred the year of President McKinley assassinated. He was president from 1897 to 1901. Theodore Roosevelt was president from 1901 to 1909. Lyman Judson Gage of Illinois was the Treasury Secretary from March 6, 1897 to January 31, 1902.

The Panic of 1907 was considered a bankers' panic. It was caused when an attempt to corner the market on United Cooper Co.'s stock failed. Many banks and trusts companies suffered because of the losses like Knickerbockers Trust Company. The panic was eased by Treasury Secretary Cortelyou depositing treasury funds in national banks and buying government bonds. J.P. Morgan also invested his money and convinced other bankers to invest also. Senator Nelson W. Aldrich established a commission to investigate which led to the creation of the Federal Reserve System. Theodore Roosevelt was the president at the time. He was considered as the anti-monopolist president. Leslie Mortimer Shaw took over as Treasury Secretary from February 1, 1902 to March 3, 1907. Then George Bruce Cortelyou became the next Treasury Secretary from March 4, 1907 to March 7, 1909.

The Panic of 1910-1911 was caused by the Sherman Anti-Trust Act being enforced. This act opposed the combination of entities that could potentially harm competition by unmerited monopolies. The panic affected the business and stock traders who were hurting due to the breakup of the Standard Oil Company. This act was signed by President Benjamin Harrison in 1890, after passing in the House and the Senate. The Sherman Anti-Trust Act is named after Republican Senator John Sherman, chairman of the Senate Finance Committee. William Taft was the president from 1909 to 1913. Franklin Mac-Veagh of Illinois was the Treasury Secretary from March 8, 1909 to March 5, 1913.

The recession of 1918 was a post World War I recession. It was caused by the end of the war production. Large number of troops returning home caused high unemployment in the labor force. Hyper-inflation in Europe due to the war caused over production in North America. The recession was short but severe. It lasted for three years. Woodrow Wilson was the president from1913 to 1921. Carter Glass of Virginia was the Secretary of the Treasury from December 16, 1918 to February 1, 1920. William Gibbs McAdoo was the secretary before Glass from March 6, 1913 to December 15, 1918. David Franklin Houston came after him as the Secretary of the Treasury.

The Great Depression of 1929 was attributed to falling real estate value, declines in the commercial and industrial sectors, and the collapse of the stock market. The stock market collapse occurred do to not having trading regulations and excessive speculation in the marketplace. The banks collapse in the United States started a global downturn which lasted for ten years. Many people placed the responsibility of the crash on the banks for putting their money at risk in the stock market. The decline in stock prices caused bankruptcies and severe economic problems, massive unemployment, home foreclosures, and business closures.

From 1923 to 1929 Calvin Coolidge was president. Commerce Secretary Herbert Hoover properly warned Coolidge of the troubles to come but he would be blamed for the depression once he was elected president. Most historians and economists should look at the policies of the previous presidents. Calvin Coolidge was at the end of his term as president. Hoover was president from 1929 to 1933. Franklin D. Roosevelt was the president from 1933-1945. Andrew William Mellon was the Treasury Secretary from March 4, 1921 to February 12, 1932. Ogden Livingston Mills, Jr. was secretary from February 13, 1932 to March 4, 1933. William Hartman Woodin was secretary from March 5, 1933 to December 31, 1933. Then Henry Morgenthau, Jr. was the Treasury Secretary from January 1, 1934 to July 22, 1945.

The recession of 1953 started around April of that year due to inflation in 1951 after the Korean War. Then more revenue was transferred into national security expanding the inflation in 1952. The monetary policy was tightened in 1952 to stop inflation by the Federal Reserve. This recession began at the end of President Truman term, from 1945-1953, lasting only a year. Dwight D. Eisenhower was president from 1953 to 1961. John Wesley Snyder was the Treasury Secretary from June 25, 1946 to January 20, 1953. George Magoffin Humphrey was the secretary at the start of the recession. He was Treasury Secretary from January 21, 1953 to July 29, 1957.

Recession of 1957 was caused by the easing of the monetary policy set two years prior. The budget balance in 1957 had a surplus of .8% GDP (Gross Domestic Product). The easing of the policy affected the budget balance in 1958 resulting in deficit of .6% of GDP. This recession hit three world economies the hardest because a decline in buying agricultural and mineral by developed countries. Dwight D. Eisenhower was president during this one-year recession. George Magoffin Humphrey of Ohio was Treasury Secretary at that time. Robert Bernard Anderson became secretary July29, 1957 to January 20, 1961 replacing him.

The recession of 1960 occured during the end of President Eisenhower term. Robert Bernard Anderson was the Secretary of the Treasury at that time. After John F. Kennedy became president, Clarence Douglass Dillion became the Treasury Secretary under him. On January 30, 1961 he increased spending to reduce unemployment. By doing so the recession ended in February. John F. Kennedy was president from 1961 to 1963. He was assassinated in 1963.

The 1973-1974 stock market crash and 1973 oil crisis lasted almost two years from January 1973 to December 1974. The stock market crash occurred due to the collapse of the Breton Woods system and the United States dollar devaluing under the Smithsonian Agreement, also with the high spending due to the Vietnam War.

OPEC (Organization of Arab Petroleum Exporting Countries) started an oil embargo in October of 1973 in response to United States support of Israel during the Yom Kippur war. The members of OPEC used their power to stabilize their incomes by quadrupling the world price of oil. Richard Nixon was the president at the time. His term was from 1969-1974. Gerald R. Ford was president from 1974 to 1977. George Pratt Shultz was Treasury Secretary from June 12, 1972 to May 8, 1974. William Edward Simon was secretary from May 8, 1974 to January 20, 1977 serving under President Nixon and Ford.

The recession of 1980 was carried over from the previous ten years of inflation. OPEC again increased the price of oil in the mid-seventies. An energy crisis began in 1979 due to the Iranian Revolution; oil was exported inconsistently at lower levels and at higher prices. Changes were made to tighten the monetary policy to control inflation which leads to another recession. This recession lasted two years. Jimmy Cater was president from 1977 to 1981. Ronald W. Reagan was president from 1981 to1989. W. Michael Blumenthal and George William Miller were the Treasury Secretaries under President Carter. Blumenthal served as secretary from January 23, 1977 to August 4, 1979 and Miller served as secretary from August 7, 1979 to January 20, 1981.

October 1987 was called Black Monday. The stock market collapsed due to saving and loans failure. The stock market collapse put a lot of American savings in jeopardy. The stock market recovered lasting for six months. Ronald Reagan was the President and James Baker III was the Treasury Secretary.

The panic that occurred after the six-month collapse led to a recession. The economy was growing, but energy and the housing market were failing. With the starting of Gulf War in the 1990, the price of oil increased. Inflation, high unemployment, and a large budget deficit had the recession lasting until 1992. Ronald W. Reagan was the president doing some of that time. George H.W. Bush was president from 1989-1993. Nicholas Brady was the Treasury Secretary from September 15, 1988 to January 17, 1993.

The Recession of 2001 started in March of that year. It was caused by the down turn of the dot- com companies and the terrorist attacks on September 11. There were massive layoffs along with companies shipping jobs over seas for cheaper labor. Many professional people had to take low paying jobs. Large Corporations were caught up in accountant misdeeds.

The recession was recorded as lasting between 6 to 8 months. It occurred at the very beginning of George W. Bush first term as president. Some considered President Clinton to be responsible for the recession. George W. Bush the son of George H.W. Bush was president from2001 to 2008. Paul H. O'Neill was the Secretary of the Treasury from January 20, 2001 to December 31, 2002.

The Bush administration left out budget deficit information findings in the 2004 annual budget reports published in February of 2003. O'Neill also had disagreements with Bush administration policies on Iraq resigning in 2002; he was replaced by John Snow.

The recession of 2007 was caused by financial greed in the real estate industry. Deregulating of credit practices for home loans and corporate loans with the subprime lending and the credit default swaps. Large world investment companies and bank suffered extreme losses. They had to deal with bankruptcy or go out of business.

Oil prices soared which in turns increased the price of food via transportation costs. Economists felt that there will be no end to this downturn. They felt that maybe we can recover by 2011. But the government started giving bailout money to large corporate banks and insurances companies near the end of 2008. Under President Obama administration, they continue with the bailout plan trying to stabilize.

We are starting to see some recover in the stock market but the unemployment rates are still high. We just have to wait and see. George W. Bush was the president from 2001 to 2008. Barack H. Obama became the president 2008 to present. Henry M. Paulson, Jr. was the Secretary of the Treasury from July 10, 2006 to January 20, 2009. Timothy F. Geithner is the present Treasury Secretary dealing with downturn in the economy at this time.

# References:


Wall Street: A History by Charles Geisst

The Presidency of John Adams (1988) by Ralph Brown

Honest John Adams (1933) by Gilbert Chinard

The Age of Federalism (1993) by Stanley M. Elkins and Eric McKitrick

Adams vs. Jefferson: The Tumultuous Election of 1800 (2004) by John Ellis

John Adams: A Life (1992) by John Ferling

John Adams: Party of One (2005) James Grant

John Adams and the Prophets of Progress (1952) Zoltan Haraszti

The Presidency of John Adams: The Collapse of Federalism, 1795-1800 (1957) by Stephen G. Kurtz

John Adams (2002) by David McCullough

The Federalist Era: 1789-1801 (1960) by John C. Miller

Adams vs. Jefferson: the tumultuous election of 1800 by John Ferling

Life of Albert Gallatin by Henry Adams

The Gallatin Divergence by Neil L. Smith

The Panic of 1819 by Murray Rothbard

A History of Money and Banking in the United States: the Colonial Era to World War II by Murray N. Rothbard

A Program for Monetary Stability by Milton Friedman

The Bank of the United States and the American Economy by Edward S Kaplan

The Panic of 1837: Some financial problems of the Jacksonian era by Reginald C. MacGran

The Panic of 1857 and the Coming of the Civil War by James L. Huston

Battle Cry of Freedom: The Civil War Era by James M. McPherson

Grant by Jean Edward Smith

A Short History of Reconstruction 1863-1877 by Eric Foner

Grover Cleveland: A Study in Courage by Allan Nevins

The Tariff Question in the Gilded Age: The Great Debate of 1888 by Joanne R. Reitano

America in the Gilded Age by Sean Cashman

Ohio and Its People by George Knepper

The Rise of Big Business, 1860-1920 by Glenn Porter

A Monetary History of the United States, 1867-1960 by Milton Friedman and Anna Jacobson Schwartz

Financial History of the United States by David R Dewey

American Radicalism, 1865-1901 by Chester McArthur Destler

William Gibbs McAdoo: A Passion for Change, 1863-1917 by John J. Broesamle

Crowded Years: The Reminiscences of William G. McAdoo by McAdoo

Alchemy of Bones: Chicago's Lugtgert Murder case of 1897 by Robert Loerzel

Rainbow's End: The Crash of 1929 by Maury Klein

1929: The Year of the Great Crash by William K. Klingaman

The Forgotten Man by Amity Shlaes

Taxation: The People's Business by Andrew W. Mellon

Economic Issues of the 1960's by Alvin H. Hansen

"Turmoil and Triumph: My Years as Secretary of States" by George P. Shultz

Back from the Brink: Greenspan Years by Steven K. Beckner

Economic Policy and the Great Stagflation by Alan s. Blinder

1959-Global financial meltdown: how we can avoid the next economic crisis by Colin Read

Encyclopedia of the Presidents and their Times by David Rubel

# Facts That Your Teacher May Know Or Maybe Not

## INTRODUCTION

I have written this book to inspire teachers and young people to speak openly and truthfully about world history. By doing so maybe I can help a young person achieve his or her dream by seeing the truth. Exposing the lies will liberate the minds of the students and the teachers.

## FIRST HUMAN BEING AND CIVILIZATION

Theories claim ancient Mesopotamia, modern day Iraq to be the first civilization to come into existence. How is that when human development dates back to 7 million years or earlier? Africans developed the first tools, fishing, astronomy, jewelry, mathematics, crops, art, and animal domestication.

Just to name a few things not shown to you in school. The Egyptians developed a calendar regulated by the sun and the moon around 4500 BC. Also in 4000 BC the technique of smelting gold and silver using copper alloys was being done in places like Egypt and Babylon

The area that the skeletal remains were found was called Kush originally. Egyptians called the land Ta-Sety. The Romans called the land Nubia derived from an Egyptian word for gold, nebew. The name Aethiopia (Ethiopia) came much later from the ancient Greek literature. The Greeks called them Ethiopians and called Nubia the Land of Punts (The Land of God).

Kush what is now Sudan and Ethiopia was the point of focus for cultural and early development of civilization. It was bountiful in natural resources such as gold, ivory, copper, and ebony. Nubia is believed to be one of the earliest cultures.

## ONE OF THE GREATEST MILITARY LEADERS IN HISTORY

Hannibal was born 247 BC in Carthage located in North Africa. Carthage was the Mediterranean's most prosperous seaport and possessed wealthy provinces. After suffering severe losses to the Romans in the First Punic War from 264-241 BC, Carthage lost its most important province, Sicily. Then civil war broke out in Carthage giving Rome the opportunity to seize Sardinia and Corsica.

Hamilcar Barca, the general of the Carthaginians, went to Iberia in 237. He needed to add new territories to the empire to compensate for the losses of the territory overseas to the Romans. He took his son Hannibal who was ten years old at the time. Hamilcar made Hannibal swear eternal hatred toward the Romans.

Hamilcar died in 229 BC, and his son-in-law Hasdrubal took command. Hasdrubal improved Carthaginian position through diplomatic means. He was murdered in 221 eight years later. Hannibal was elected commander of Carthaginian by the soldiers and the government confirmed it. He was a twenty-six-year-old general.

Hannibal in following his father military style he captured Salamanca a city in Western Spain. He also captured Saguntum after an eight-month standoff. Saguntum (modern Sagunto) is a city in eastern Spain. It was a Roman ally. In capturing Saguntum Rome felt that it was a violation of the treaty between Hasdrubal his brother-in-law and the Roman Republic.

The Roman government demanded that the Carthaginian government turn over Hannibal to them. While they were trying to reach agreement on him, he extends his country's territory. Hannibal made his brother Hasdrubal who has the same name as their brother-in-law who was murdered. He made him the commander in Iberia which is now modern-day Spain and Portugal so he could continue the conquering of Iberia completely.

Rome declared the Second Punic War. Hannibal decided to invade Italy before the Romans could prepare. Hannibal crossed the Pyrenees and the river Rhone ferrying 50,000 soldiers, 9,000 cavalry and 37 elephants. He crossed the Alps through the snow.

Hannibal reached the plains along the river Po October 218. He had 38,000 soldiers, 8,000 cavalry and not many elephants. Rome sent an army to prevent Hannibal of becoming allies with the Gaul's. Roman army was defeated and 14,000 Gauls volunteered to join Hannibal. He won the second battle at the river Trebia with the help of the Gauls.

Hannibal won many battles against the Romans and almost conquest Italy. He also aided many other countries in his flight from Rome. It came to an end at his hands. Hannibal poisoned himself to avoid capture in the winter of 183 or 182.

He was a military genius his military techniques were adopted by his enemies and studied by many military leaders to this day.


## WHO DISCOVERED THE AMERICAS?

The first native America made the difficult journey across the ice from Siberia to Alaska, between 12,000-10,00 0BC when the two land masses were connected. They gradually moved down the west coast of the Continent spreading eastward until they eventually occupied the whole continent of north and South America.

These Native American people effectively advanced to become sophisticated civilizations mainly in the tropical regions. They were the Inca and Maya to name a few.

## WHO SAILED TO THE CONTINENT OF THE AMERICAS FIRST?

Egyptian imported gold by sailing the Nile around 2300 BC. They also traveled across the Atlantic about 2000 BC on papyrus boats and landed in what is now Central America. The Egyptians' journey occurred before the Vikings and long before Christopher Columbus. It is believed that trade between West African and the Native Americans started as early as 30,000 BC or earlier.

## WHO WAS THE FIRST PRESIDENT OF THE UNITED STATES OF AMERICA?

George Washington was not the first president of the United States. He was actually the eighth president. He was the first president under the Constitution. John Hanson was the first president of the United States. The United States was truly formed on March 1, 1781 under the Articles of Confederation.

John Hanson was a brilliant administrator as a congressman from 1777 to his president. He was elected president in 1781. He served as president from November 5, 1781 to November 3, 1782 which was a full term under the Articles of Confederation.

President is allowed to serve only one year term during a three-year time period under the Article of Confederation. John Hanson was elected unanimously by Congress which George Washington was a member. He took office at the end of the Revolutionary War. His role was not fully defined. He had no blueprint to follow since there had never been a president. He had to pay the soldiers after the long war which he did. He established the Great Seal of the United States which is used on all official documents to this day.

President Hanson started the first Treasury and Foreign Affairs Departments. He also established the first Secretary of War. He declared the fourth Thursday of November to be Thanksgiving Day which is the same too today. He was born 1715 and died in 1783.

Who Was the Father of Medicine, Architecture and Engineering?

Imhotep was known as the father of medicine, architecture and engineering. He designed the Step Pyramids in Egypt between 2630-2611 BC. He also authored medical papyrus containing ailments and cures, and also anatomical observations. The Greeks and Romans worshipped him as a god through the Greco-Roman periods. He is believed to have been born in Memphis, Egypt.

## WHO DEVELOPED THE FIRSTS IN AGRICULTURE?

Egyptians developed first tools for plowing and raking around 3500 BC. Egyptians and the Sumerians grew barley used in the making of bread and beer around 3000 BC. In 2100 BC, Peruvians were cultivating cotton around that time.

I feel in giving you some of these brief facts it will inspire you to seek the truth and become more informed about what is fact and what is fiction.

# Presidential Assassinations and Attempted Assassinations

## 1865 to Present

THERE HAVE BEEN MULTIPLE ATTEMPTS TO ASSASSINATE present and former presidents of the United States. There were only four president assassination attempts that were successful, the assassination of Abraham Lincoln who was the 16th President, James A. Garfield our 20th President, William McKinley our 25th President and also John F. Kennedy our 35th President. We also have two, Theodore Roosevelt our 26th president and Ronald Reagan the 40th president, that were injured in there assassination attempts.

An assassination was attempted on the president while attending a funeral ceremony for Congressman Warren Davis at the Capitol January 30, 1835 by Richard Lawrence, a house painter. He pointed two flintlock derringers at President Andrew Jackson. He first aimed one of the pistols at the president standing 13 feet away and the pistol misfired. He then fired the second one at point blank range it also misfired. He was captured after being beaten by President Jackson with a cane. In court he was found not guilty by reason of insanity. He spent the rest of his life confined in a mental institution.

April 14, 1865 at 10:15 P.M., President and Mrs. Lincoln while attending performance of Our American Cousin at Ford's Theatre in Washington D.C. John Wilkes Booth, an actor and Confederate sympathizer, entered the president booth and shot the president in the back of the head. President Lincoln died the next day April 15, 1865 at 7:22 A.M. in Mr. William Petersen's home. John Wilkes Booth escaped after the shooting but was later found and was shot and killed.

President James A. Garfield's assassination took place at the train station in Washington D.C. as he waited to leave to go to a college reunion. It took place at 9:30 A.M. Saturday, July 2, 1881. Charles J. Guiteau a mentally disturbed man seeking government office approached him and fired two shots with a .442 Webley British Bulldog revolver. President Garfield lived for eleven weeks and died due to infections Friday September 19, 1881. His death was attributed more to poor medical care by the physicians than to the wounds. Charles J. Guiteau was convicted and hung for murder June 30, 1882.

President William McKinley was assassinated Friday September 6, 1901. He was shot twice by Leon Czolgosz at the Pan-American Exposition in Buffalo, New York. He died September 14, 1901. Czolgosz was convicted and electrocuted for murder October 29, 1901.

Theodore Roosevelt's assassination attempt occurred after he left office and decided to run for president once again against William Howard Taft. While campaigning in Milwaukee, Wisconsin on October 14, 1912, he was shot in the chest once with a .38 caliber revolver by John F. Schrank. Schrank was a saloonkeeper from New York. Roosevelt had a 50 page speech folded and his metal eye glass case in his breast pocket that slowed the bullet. Roosevelt gave his speech with the bullet still lodged in his chest. He later went to the hospital. He remembered President McKinley died after his operation to remove his bullets. So he chose not to have the bullet removed. John F. Schrank was found insane and he spent the rest of his life in a mental institution.

Giuseppe Zangara fired six shots into a crowd Thursday February 15, 1933 in Miami, Florida after Franklin D. Roosevelt speech. Four people were wounded and the Mayor of Chicago Anton Cermak was killed none of the shot hit Roosevelt. This attempted assassination occurred a month before Roosevelt was swore in for the first term of his Presidency. Zangara was convicted for attempted murder and once Anton Cermak died due to his wounds. Zangara was retried and convicted for murder and he was executed March 20, 1933 by electric chair.

On November 1, 1950, President Truman and his family were staying at the Blair house across the street from the White House when two Puerto Rican pro independence activists, Oscar Collazo and Griselio Torresola attempted to assassinate President Turman to bring attention to Puerto Ricans' case for independences. Collazo and Torresola tried to shoot their way into the house. The gun battle ensued between them and the Secret Service Police. Torresola wounded a White House policeman and killed the other one. White House Policeman Leslie Coffelt was able to shoot and kill Torresola before he died. Collazo was serious injured and arrested. He was sentenced to death, but President Truman commuted to life in jail. In 1979 President Carter freed Collazo from prison.

On Friday, November 22, 1963, in Dallas, Texas, at 12:30 P.M. Lee Harvey Oswald allegedly assassinated President John F. Kennedy. He fatally shot the President in the head with a high power rifle as the president, first lady and Governor John Connelly traveled in a convertible limousine to a meeting with the Citizens Council. Oswald was an employee of the Texas School Book Depository there in Dealey Plaza. He was killed two days later by Jack Ruby before he was to stand trial.

Samuel Byck tried to hijack a plane to kill President Nixon on February 22, 1974. He planned to crash the plane into the White House to kill President Nixon. He hijacked the plane but the plane could not take off with the wheel blocks in place. So he shot the pilot and the co-pilot. He was then shot through the door window by one of the officers before killing himself.

President Gerald Ford had two assassination attempts on his life. The first was September 5, 1975 in Sacramento, California, a Charles Manson follower, Lynette Squeaky Fromme, pointed a Colt .45 caliber pistol at the president but she did not have a round in the firing chamber. She was captured by a Secret Service agent. She was sentenced to life in prison. She was released August 14, 2009 nearly 34 yrs later. Then in San Francisco, California there was a second attempt on his life by Sara Jane Moore. She was trying to prove herself to a radical group. Oliver Sipple a bystander grabbed Sara arm and the shot missed the president. She was convicted and sentenced to life in prison. On Monday, December 31, 2007 she was paroled from federal prison.

Raymond Lee Harvey was arrested for carrying a gun May 5, 1979 two minutes before a presidential speech. President was to speak at the civic center mall in Los Angeles. Later he told that he and Osvaldo Ortiz were to be a diversion so that armed hit man with sniper rifles could assassinate President Carter. He was released do to lack of evidence.

President Reagan and his Press Secretary James Brady, Secret Service agent Tim McCarthy, also D.C police officer Thomas Delahanty were wounded returning to the President's limousine they all survived. Incident occurred March 30, 1981, after speech at the Hilton Washington Hotel in Washington, D.C. The President was shot in the lung and the Press Secretary James Brady was permanently disabled by John Hinckley, Jr. Hinckley was arrested and found guilty by reason of insanity. He is serving a life sentence in a mental institution.

Assassination attempt on President George H. W. Bush was foiled by Kuwaiti offices April 13, 1993. The Kuwaiti officials arrested sixteen men who smuggled a car bomb with intentions to assassinate the president as he spoke at the Kuwait University. The men were allegedly of Saddam Hussein's Iraq Intelligence Service.

There were three different assassination attempts tried on President William Jefferson Clinton: September 12, 1994 and October 29, 1994, also November 1994. First attempt was by Frank Eugene Corder who tried to fly a single-engine Cessna into the White house. He crashed the plane into the White House lawn; he was the only casualty. The second attempt was by Francisco Martin Duran; he fired about 29 shots from the White House fence at the north lawn. Three men tourists tackled Duran before anyone was injured. He was arrested and sentence to 40 years in prison.

July 2001 Robert Pickett was found to be emotional unstable. He was sentenced to three years of imprisonment for firing a weapon toward the White House standing outside the fence. The incident ended after a ten minutes stand off when a Secret Service officer shot Pickett, injuries requiring immediate hospitalization.

On May 10, 2005 in Freedom Square Tbilisi, Georgia, President George W. Bush was giving a speech. Vladimir Arutyunian threw a Soviet made hand grenade at the podium where President Bush, Georgian President Mikhail Saakashvili and also their wives seated. The grenade did not explode because a handkerchief wrapped around the grenade kept the firing pin from deploying quickly.

Three white supremacist plots to assassinate Barack Obama during the 2008 Democratic National Convention in Denver, Colorado. They were investigated after making racist threats against Obama while taking drugs in their hotel room in Hyatt Regency Tech Center. Tharin Robert Gartrell, 28 was arrested after being found with rifles and other weaponry. His cousin Shawn Robert Adolf, 33 and their friend Nathan Dwaine Johnson was arrested a short time later. Johnson identified Adolf as the organizer of the plot. To downplay the plot, the three men were charged with drug and weapons and not the assassination attempt.

# THE IRS

## The what, when, why and who started the Internal Revenue Service

P RESIDENT LINCOLN AND CONGRESS CREATED THE
office of Commissioner of Internal Revenue and enacted an income tax to pay wartime expenses. It was called the Revenue Act of
1862. It was actually passed in 1861.It was an emergency, temporary
wartime tax.

The IRS was started due to the tension of the post American Revolution tax system of trade and property taxation. The tension was
primarily between the north and the southern states. The Act was a
copy of the British system of income taxation. States versus the federal
rights was one of the causes of the Civil war. The other causes were
economic and social differences, slave and non-slave proponents, ab-
olition movement and the election of Lincoln.

After the Civil War, the incomes taxes continue to be required
for the public funding for reconstruction, and transforming the north
and the south. But in 1864 the constitutionality of the acted was question and was ruled unconstitutional by the Supreme Court. In 1872
seven years after the war lawmakers allowed the temporary Civil War
income tax to expire.

A year later the Panic of 1873 happened. It was due to the failure
of several banks September 18, 1873. The stock market closed for ten
days and the economy was in crisis. Railroad crises caused economic
overinvesting and overexpansion came from excessive construction.
Treasury Secretary Richardson issued paper money to the banks to
ease the crisis. Income taxes evolved but in 1894, in the midst of a 30-

year post-Civil War depression the Supreme Court declared the Income Tax of 1894 unconstitutional in Pollock vs. Farmers' Loan & Trust Co.

In 1906 President Theodore Roosevelt and later his successor William Howard Taft felled tax reform was necessary. Under Woodrow Wilson Congress pass the Underwood Tariff October1913, lowering the tariff rates affected the government revenue. So to recoup the losses the new law also established the first national income tax. February 1913 the ratification of the Sixteenth Amendment of the Constitution, granted Congress the right to create a direct income tax.

Sixteenth Amendment of the Constitution:

The Congress shall have power to lay and collect taxes on incomes, from whatever source derived, without apportionment among the several States, and without regard to any census or enumeration.

By February 1913, 36 states ratified the change to the Constitution. By March 6 more states had ratified the change. 42 states of the 48 states at that time ratified the change. In the first year after ratification of the Sixteenth Amendment, no taxes were actually collected. Taxpayers had to just simply complete the form and the IRS checked it for accuracy.

The purpose of the ratification of this Amendment was the direct consequence of the Court's decision in 1895 in Pollock vs. Farmers' Loan & Trust Co

The IRS Commissioner and Chief Counsel are political appointees selected by the President and confirmed by the United States Senate.

# Some
## Of
## Worst
## Vice Presidents
## In
## History

This book came about after I researched the responsibilities of the vice president. The vice president is the president of the Senate. He or she is simply the deciding vote in a tie vote and presides over trials in the Senate. The vice president office is basically ceremonial, attending ceremonies and making speeches when the president cannot. The vice president is the just in case person if the president become ill or died.

I decided to write this book so people could see that Richard Cheney may be considered the worst Vice President in history. But the field of candidates is larger than most would think here are some candidates in the order of the years they served.

Aaron Burr, Jr. was the third Vice President of the United States from March 4, 1801 to March 4, 1805. He served as Vice President under Thomas Jefferson. He was born in Newark, New Jersey, February 6, 1756.

Aaron Burr had an unsuccessful reelection for Governor of New York. Due to his defeat by Philip Schuyler whom preceded him. They were severe political rivals for a long time. Philip Schyler was also the father-in-law of the former Secretary of Treasury Alexander Hamilton. Hamilton made some remarks Burr did not like and he would not apology. So Burr challenged Hamilton to a duel at the Heights of Weehawken in New Jersey July 11, 1804 in which he killed Alexander Hamilton. He was charged with murder in New York and New Jersey. He was acquitted and the charges were dismissed this event ruin his political career.

After Burr's term of vice presidency was over, he traveled to the lands acquired in the Louisiana Purchase. Then rumors started that Burr was plotting to secede from the United States and form his own monarchy and become the emperor of the land acquired in the Louisiana Purchase. He was arrested and charged with treason, of which he was acquitted.

John C. Calhoun served from 1825 to 1833 as vice president two consecutive terms for two different presidents, John Quincy Adams and Andrew Jackson. He was a very controversial politician and an advocate of slavery. He once was a supporter of the nationalist philosophy. Once he became vice president, Calhoun opposed Adams's nationalist program and under Jackson the Tariff of 1828.

The Tariff was approved by President Jackson and Congress. Calhoun, angry and frustrated, left office and returned to his state, South Carolina. He tried to use the doctrine of nullification which states, individual states that deemed federal legislation unconstitutional could override it. Calhoun's false interposition of the doctrine of nullification states a state has the right to secede from the Union. Through his writings he nearly had South Carolina seceding the Union and on the brink of Civil War. President Jackson and Vice President Calhoun's relationship was very bad because of the vice president's political beliefs and all of the public scandals he and his wife were involved in. President Jackson was later heard saying that he regretted not having him hung. Calhoun's actions would be considering treason in my opinion.

Richard M. Johnson served as President Martin Van Buren's number two from 1800. He started in politics by trying to be a war hero. He claimed he killed Tecumseh in the war of 1812. It was never proven. He also proposed that Congress fund an expedition to the North Pole, he believed the earth to be hollow. Johnson was also a slave-owner who forced slave women as he says it to be his common-law wives. Julia Chinn was one who he inherited from his father. When she died, he grabbed others.

In 1829-1837 as a member of the House of Representatives, Johnson pushed for a bill to end debtor's prison. He was often in debt himself. President Van Buren grew tried of Johnson by 1840. Johnson served just one term as vice president.

Schuyler Colfax, Jr. served as Vice president from March 4, 1869 to March 4, 1873 under President Ulysses S. Grant. Grant's administration was corrupt with more than a dozen government officials including Vice president Colfax. The vice president was involved in the Credit Mobilier of America scandal where Union-Pacific Railroad stocks for construction contracts were accepted by him. He was left off the ticket for the running for a second term. On January 13, 1885 Schuyler Colfax died of a heart attack cause by walking three-fourths of a mile in minus 30 degree weather to change trains.

Spiro Agnew was President Richard Nixon Vice president from 1969-1973. Agnew was the second Vice President to resign the office. John C Calhoun resigned to take a seat in the Senate. Vice President Agnew resigned October 10, 1973 in negotiating plead of no contest to tax evasion and money laundering bribes during his time of being governor of Maryland.

Dick Cheney was vice president under George W Bush from January 20, 2001 to January 20, 2009 from Wyoming. Dick Cheney misused his office in ways other vice presidents could not have imagined. He made his office a second White House with policy advisers and lawyers. He was a key member in planning Iraq and the environment policy. He felt that the vice president is not a part of the executive branch.

So now knowing a little about some of the vice presidents you can decide the worst vice president in the U.S. history. Aaron Burr shot and killed Hamilton. Andrew Jackson was a drunkard. Elbridge Gerry was a philanderer and an adulterer. Richard M. Johnson was a rapist. Schuyler Colfax, Jr. and Agnew both were white collard criminals. Cheney was most of these things. He shot his friend hunting. Some considered him a philanderer and a white collared criminal through his connection to a company like Halliburton.

# REFERENCES


*Fallen Founder: The Life of Aaron Burr* by Nancy Isenberg

*Life of Elbridge Gerry* by James Austin

*Masters without Slaves: Southern Planters in the Civil War and Reconstruction* by James L. Roark

*Life of Schuyler Colfax* by James O. Hollister

*Witness to Power: The Nixon Years* by J. Ehrlichmann

*Angler: The Cheney Vice Presidency* by Barton Gellman

*Encyclopedia of the Presidents and Their Times* by David Rubel